What's New?

written by Judy Nayer • illustrated by Sarah Beise

Macmillan
McGraw-Hill
New York Farmington

Something new is happening at our house.

Do you know what it is?

My sisters know.

They're getting everything ready.

Do you know?

My brothers know.

They're getting everything ready.

Do you know?

My dad knows.

He's getting things ready too.

Do you know?

My mom knows. She's ready!

She's ready to go!

My dad goes with her.

Now do you know?

It's a baby!

We have a new baby at our house!